JAMIE CULLUM THE PURSUIT

PIANO
VOCAL
GUITAR

T0061350

ISBN 978-1-4234-9017-3

HAL•LEONARD®
CORPORATION
7777 W. BLUEMOUND RD. P.O. BOX 13819 MILWAUKEE, WI 53213

Visit Hal Leonard Online at
www.halleonard.com

JUST ONE OF THOSE THINGS

Words and Music by
COLE PORTER

Moderately fast Swing (♩♩=♩♪)

It was just

one of those things,

just ___ one of those ___ cra - zy flings, _

one of those bells

that now and then rings,

one of those things.   It was just_____

one of those nights,

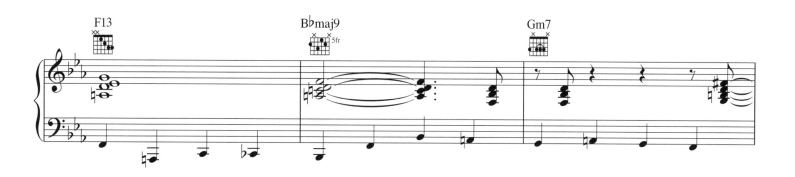

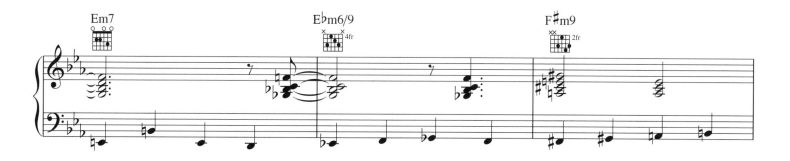

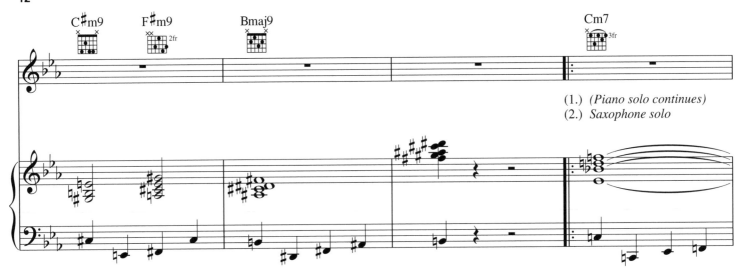

(1.) (Piano solo continues)
(2.) Saxophone solo

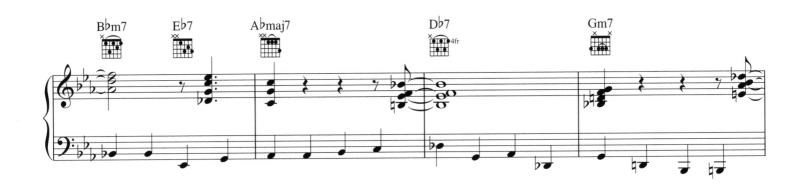

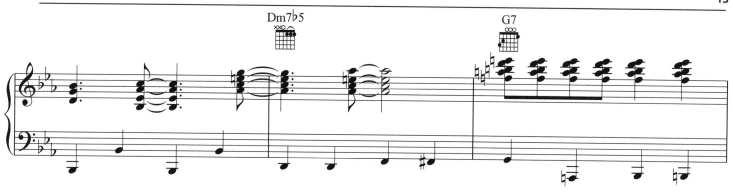

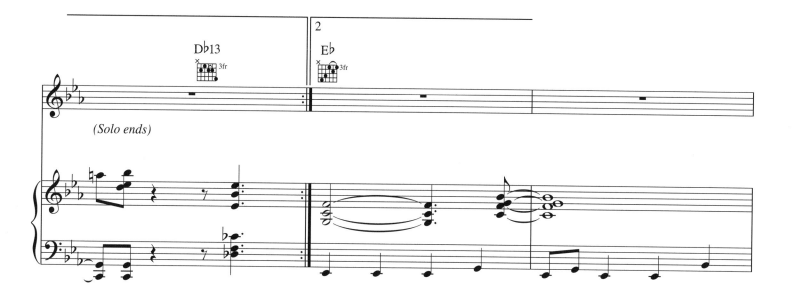

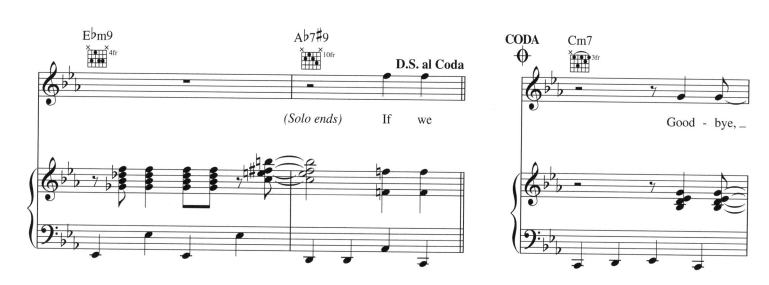

I'M ALL OVER IT

Words and Music by JAMIE CULLUM
and RICKY ROSS

Moderate Shuffle

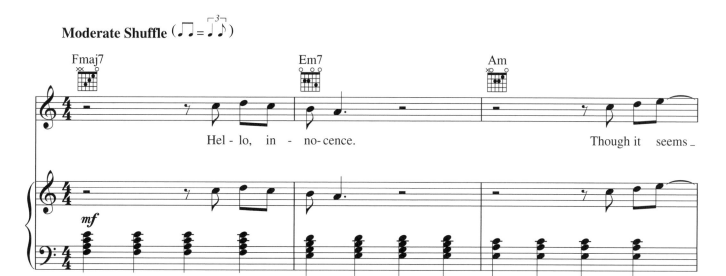

Hel-lo, in-no-cence. Though it seems

like we've been friends for years, I'm fin-ish-ing.

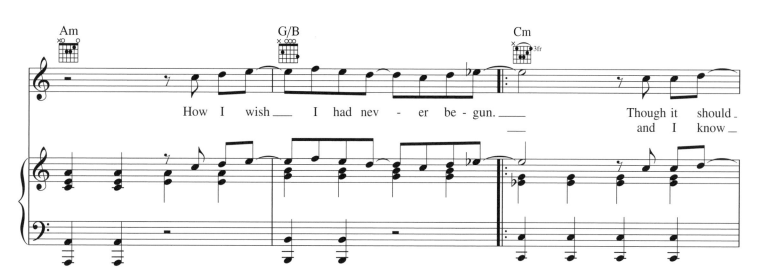

How I wish I had nev-er be-gun.
and I know

Though it should

WHEELS

Words and Music by JAMIE CULLUM
and BEN CULLUM

* Recorded a half step lower.

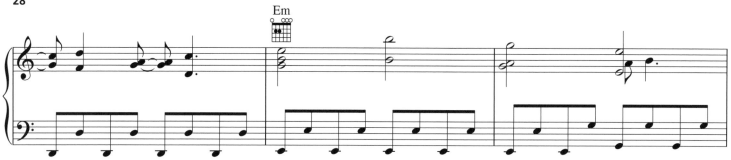

The wheels ___ are fall - ing off the world. _

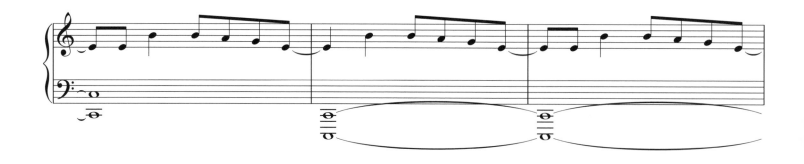

IF I RULED THE WORLD

Words by LESLIE BRICUSSE
Music by CYRIL ORNADEL

Moderately slow

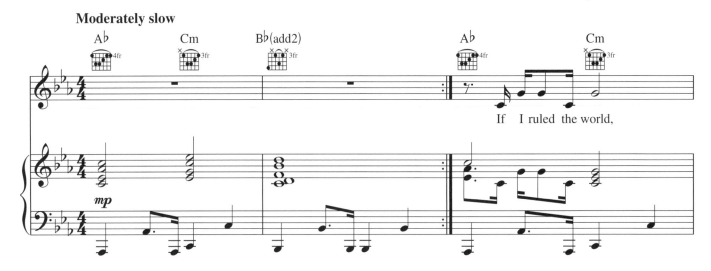

If I ruled the world,

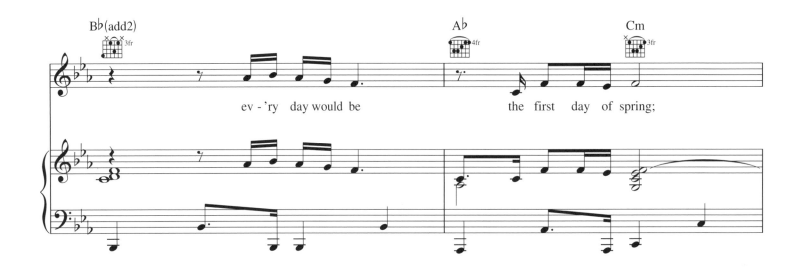

ev-'ry day would be   the first day of spring;

ev-'ry heart _____ would have a   new song _____ to sing, ____

(Solo ends)

If I ruled the world, ___ ev-'ry man would see the world was his

friend, ___ yeah. _____ There'd be ___ hap-pi-ness that no ___

man ___ could end. ___ No, my friend,

world.

Ev-'ry head would be held up high. The stars shine down on us too, if the day ev-er dawned

when I ruled the world.

rit.

YOU AND ME ARE GONE

Words and Music by JAMIE CULLUM,
GEOFF GASCOYNE and SEBASTIAAN DE KROM

Ev-'ry time ___
Truth-ful - ly, ___

___ I see ___ what's writ - ten on ___ your mind, ___
___ I've got ___ a mo - dus op - er - and...

* Recorded one step lower.

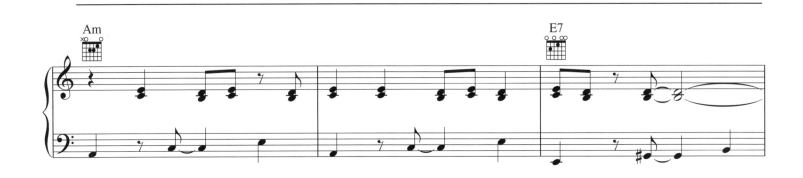

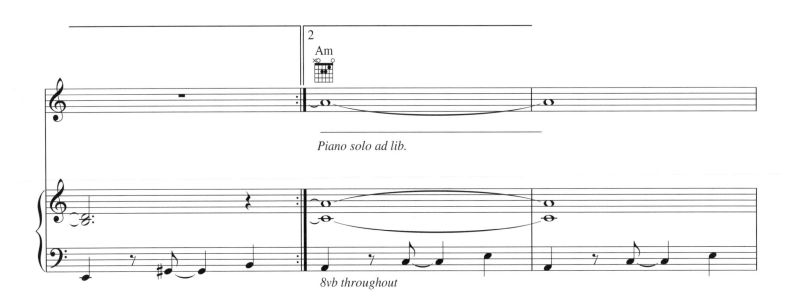

Piano solo ad lib.

8vb throughout

Seems that joy -

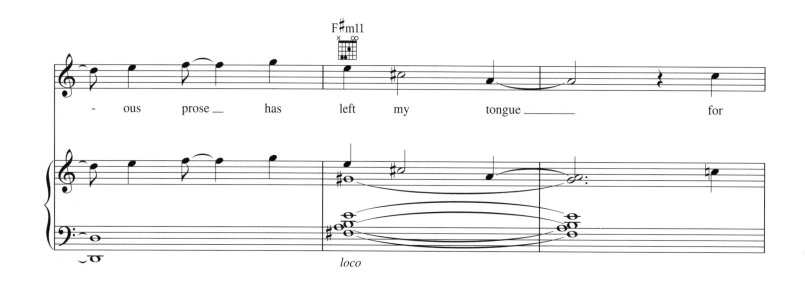

- ous prose __ has left my tongue _____ for

loco

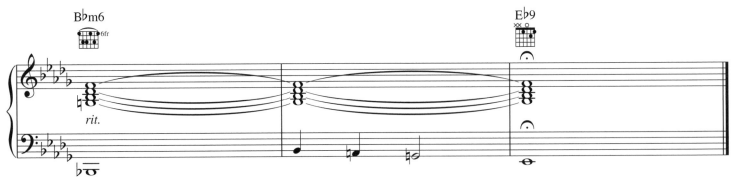

DON'T STOP THE MUSIC

Words and Music by TOR ERIK HERMANSEN,
FRANKIE STORM, MIKKEL ERIKSEN
and MICHAEL JACKSON

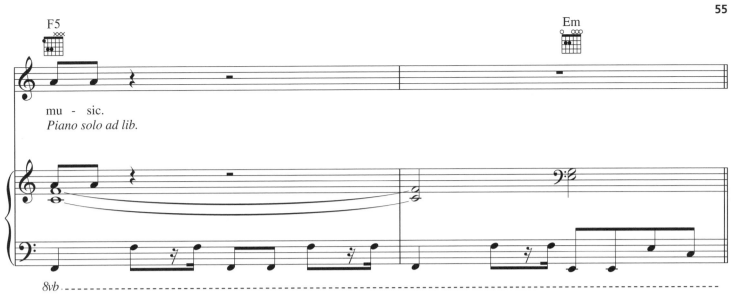

mu - sic.
Piano solo ad lib.

8vb

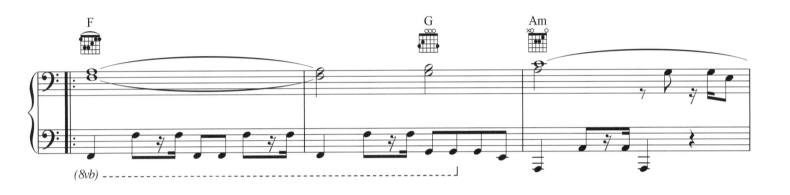

(8vb)

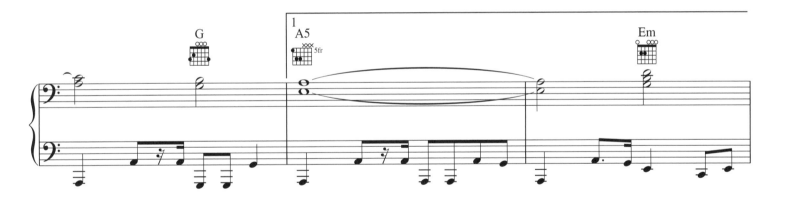

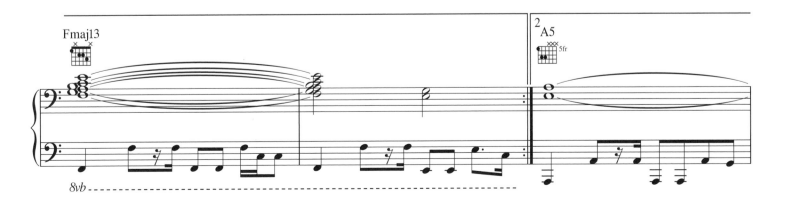

8vb

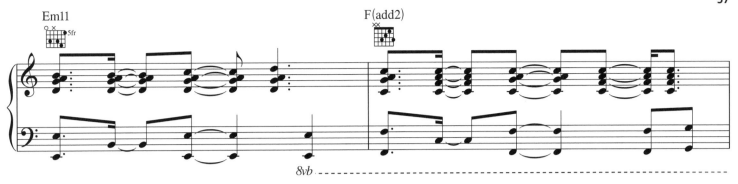

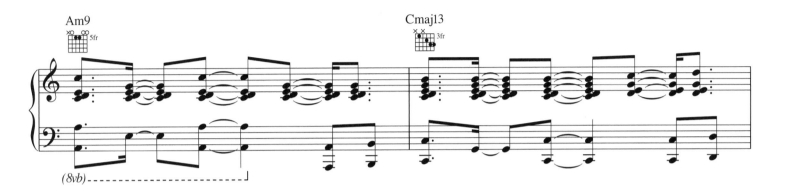

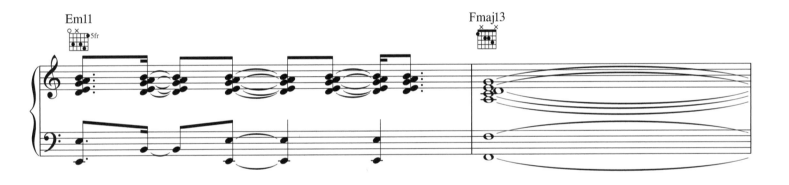

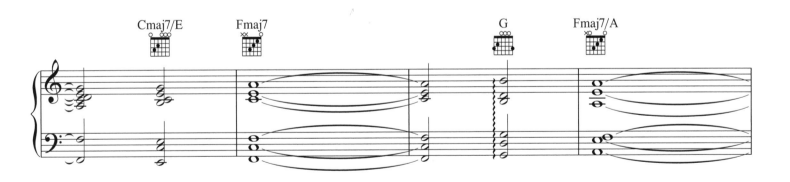

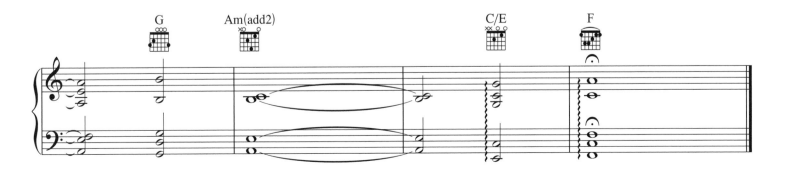

LOVE AIN'T GONNA LET YOU DOWN

Words and Music by
JAMIE CULLUM

* *Recorded a half step lower.*

MIXTAPE

Words and Music by JAMIE CULLUM
and BEN CULLUM

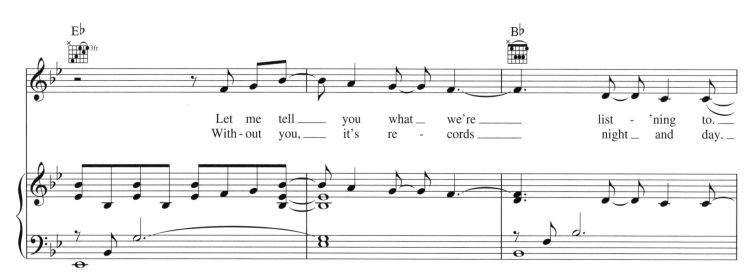

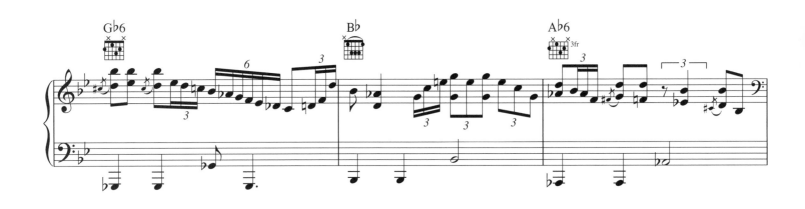

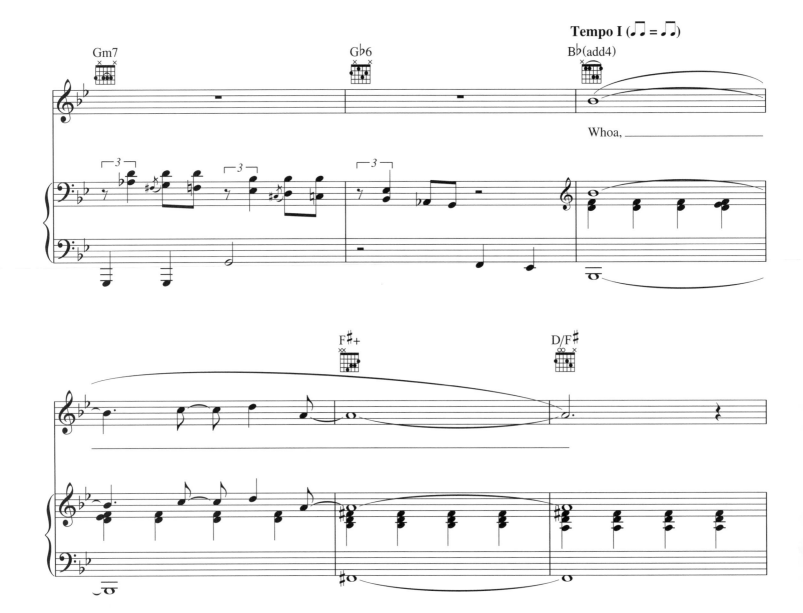

Tempo I ($\sqrt{} = \sqrt{}$)

Whoa,

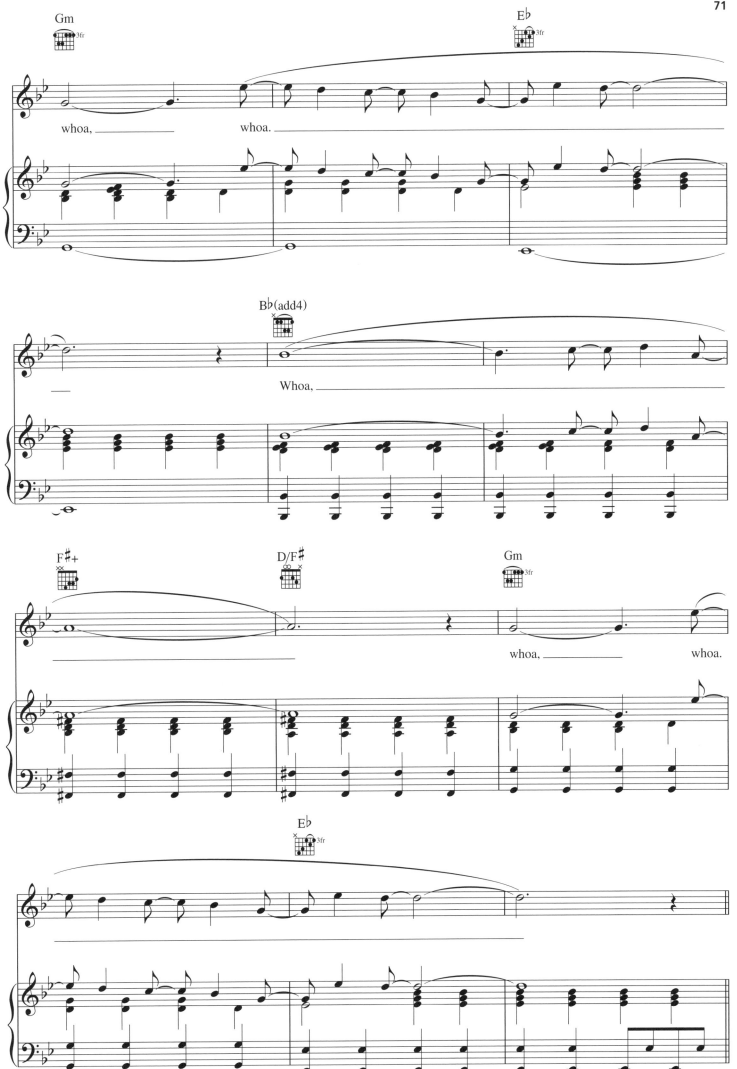

Whoa,

whoa,

whoa.

Repeat and Fade

Optional Ending

rit.

I THINK, I LOVE

Words and Music by
JAMIE CULLUM

WE RUN THINGS

Words and Music by JAMIE CULLUM,
BEN CULLUM and KARL GORDON JR.

(1., 2.) We run things an - oth - er way. We run things an - oth - er way. ___ {Ya I

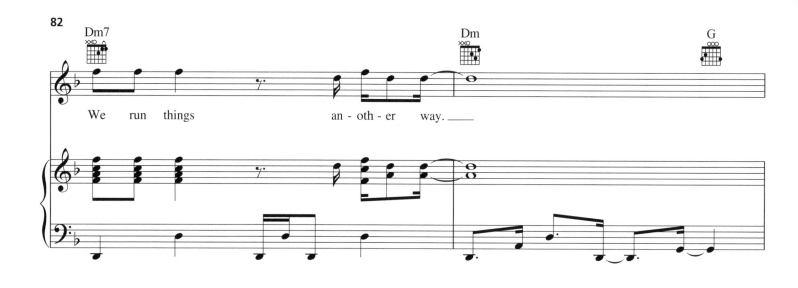

We run things   an - oth - er   way. ____

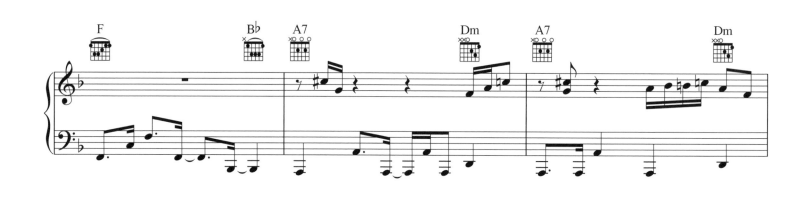

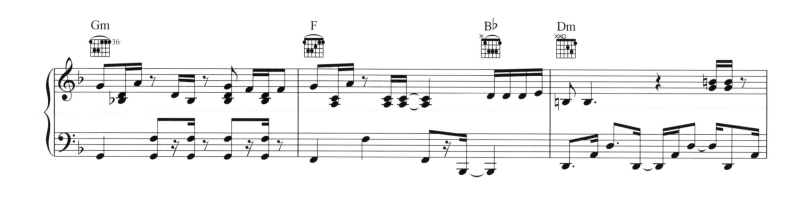

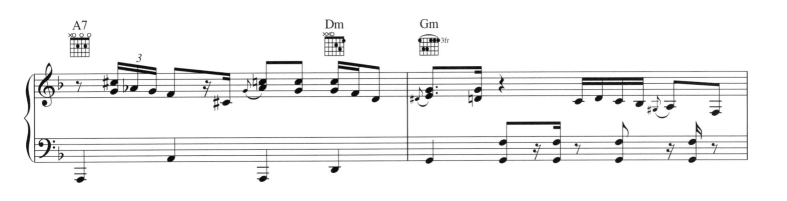

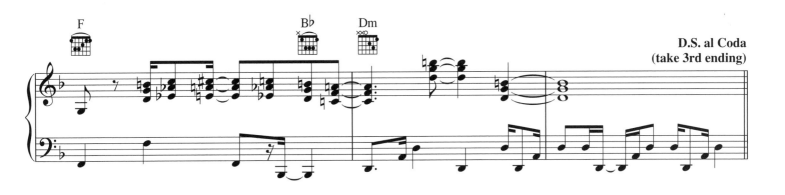

D.S. al Coda
(take 3rd ending)

We run things an-oth-er way.____ We run things... I'm

NOT WHILE I'M AROUND

Words and Music by
STEPHEN SONDHEIM

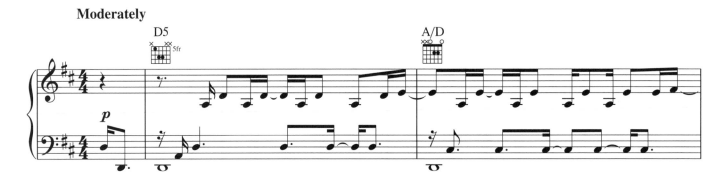

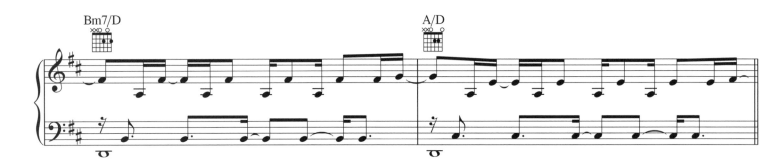

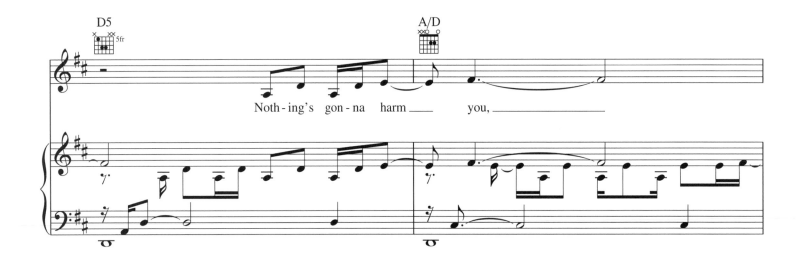

Noth-ing's gon-na harm ____ you, ____

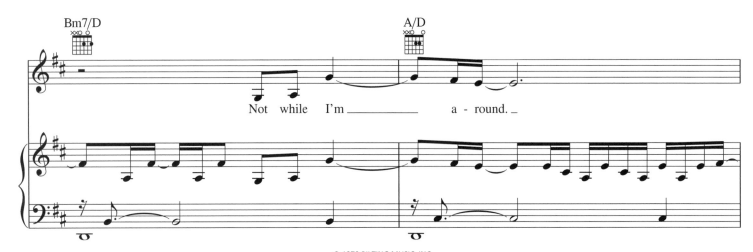

Not while I'm ____ a - round. _

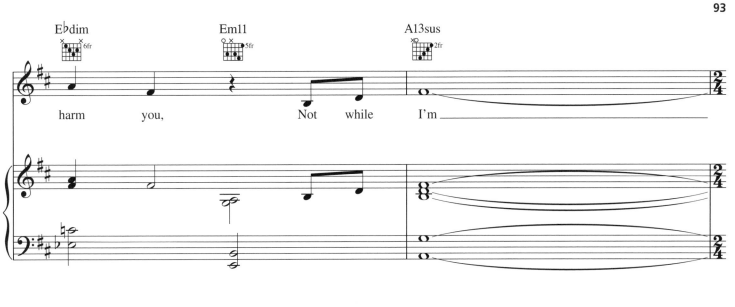

harm   you,   Not   while   I'm _____

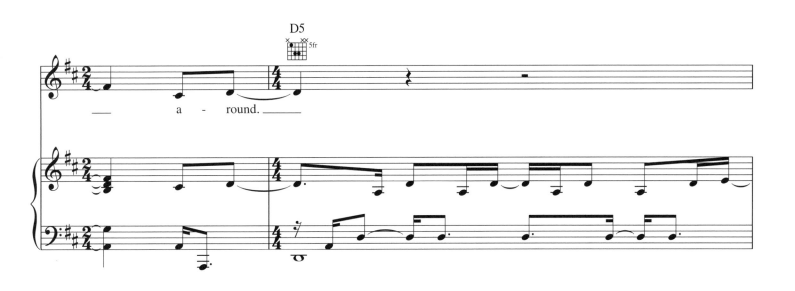

___ a - round. _____

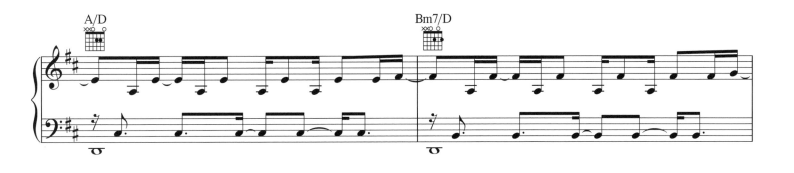

rit.

MUSIC IS THROUGH

Words and Music by JAMIE CULLUM
and BEN CULLUM

Moderately fast

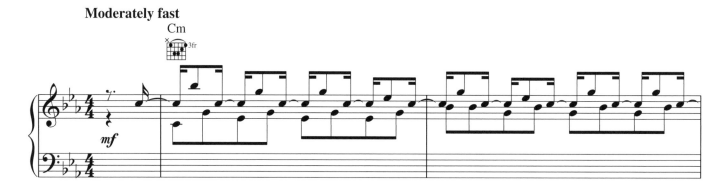

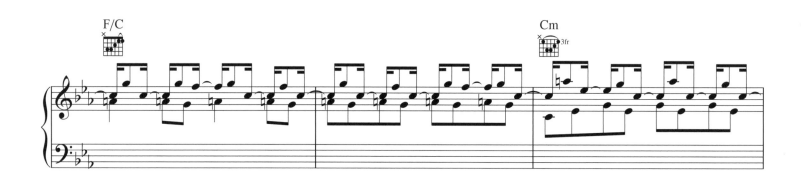

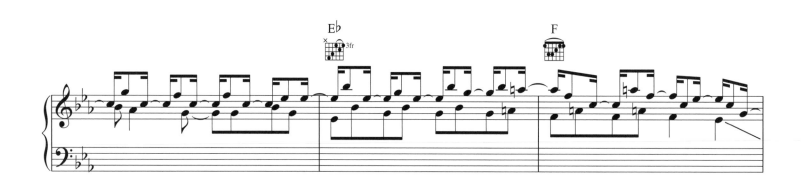

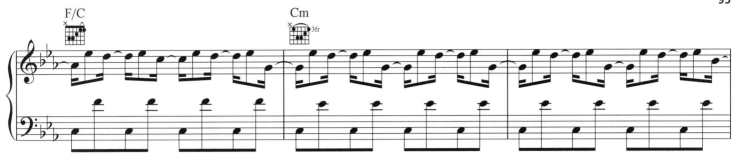

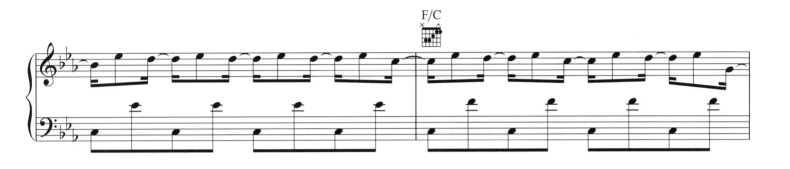

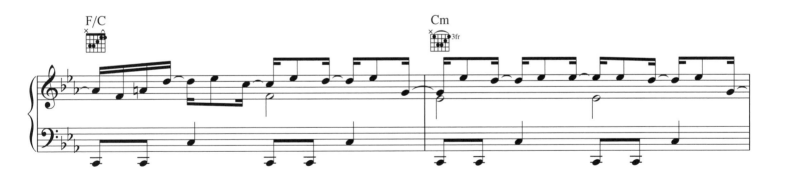

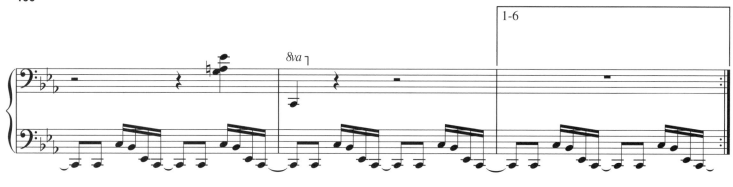

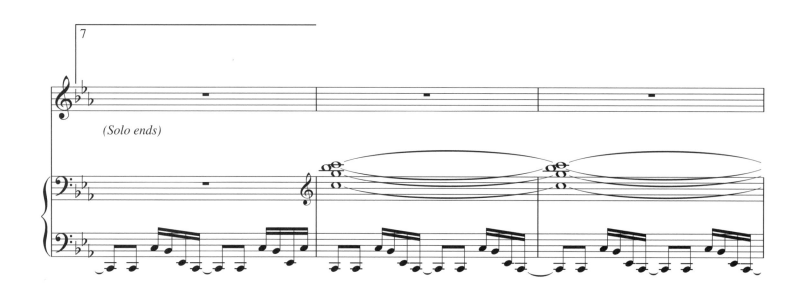

(Solo ends)

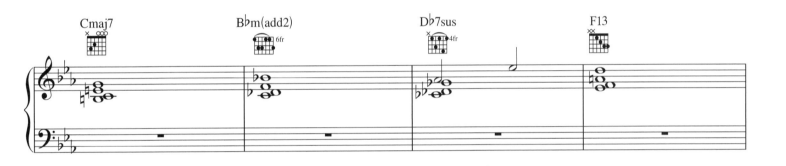

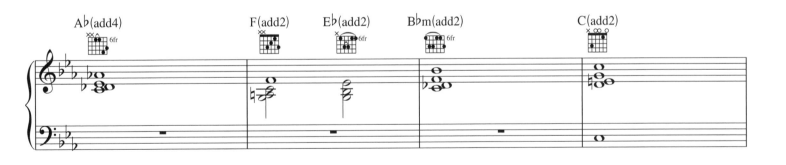

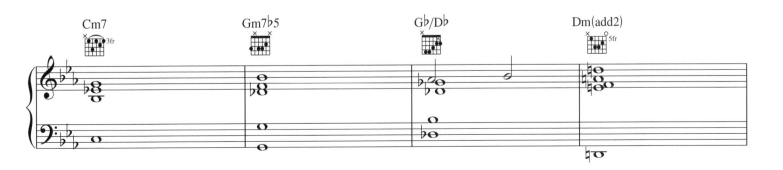

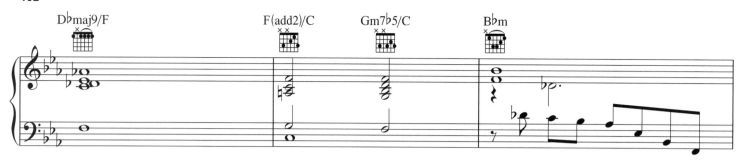

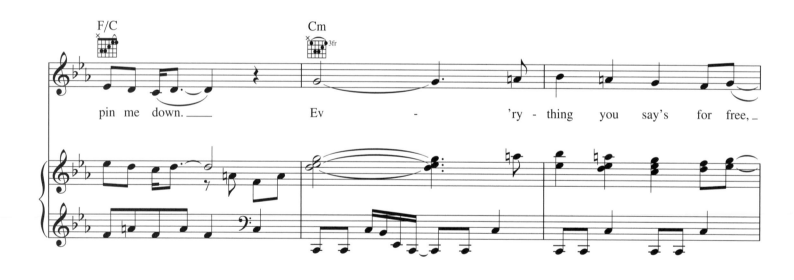

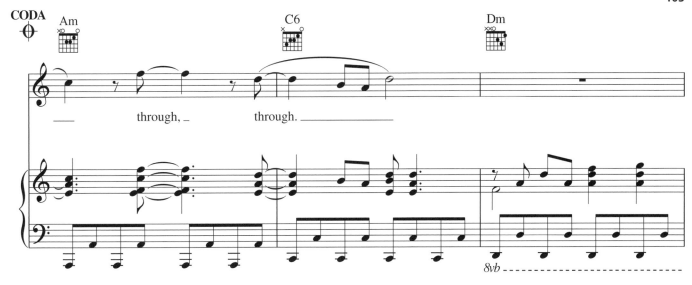

through, _ through. _____

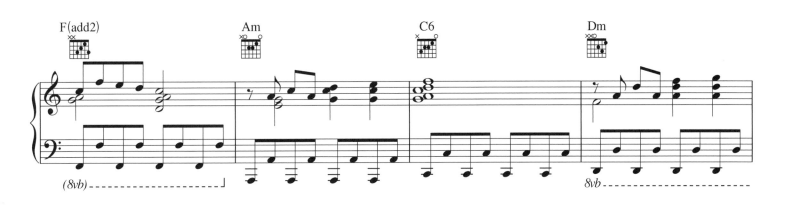

Girl, I got your num - ber, call you when the mu - sic is through. _____

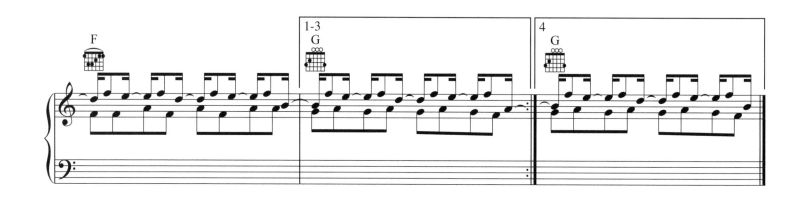

I GET ALONG WITHOUT YOU VERY WELL
(Except Sometimes)

Words and Music by HOAGY CARMICHAEL
Inspired by a poem written by J.B. THOMPSON

EVERYONE'S LONELY

Words and Music by JAMIE CULLUM
and BEN CULLUM

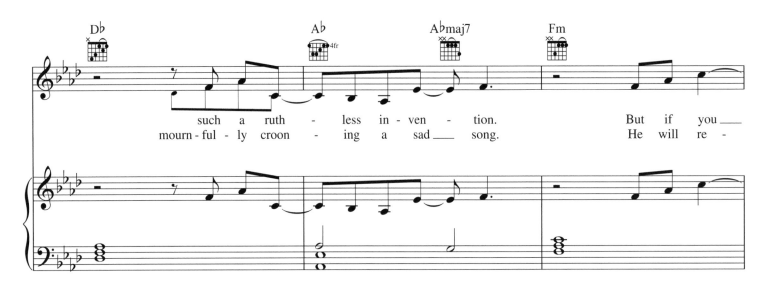

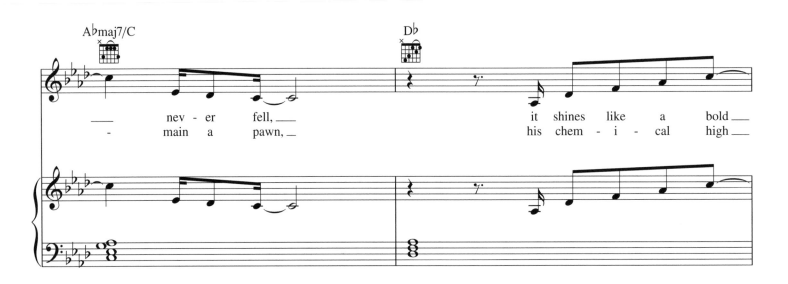

GRACE IS GONE

Words and Music by CAROLE BAYER SAGER
and CLINT EASTWOOD

Recorded a half step higher.

GRAN TORINO

Words and Music by JAMIE CULLUM,
CLINT EASTWOOD, KYLE EASTWOOD
and MICHAEL STEVENS

D.S. al Coda

128